CONSERVING WATER

Water Wise

Gail Parman

PowerKiDS press.

Published in 2027 by
The Rosen Publishing Group, Inc.
2544 Clinton Street, Buffalo, NY 14224

Designer: Beeline Media and Design
Editor: Tricia Hoffman

Portions of this work were originally authored by Peter Castellano and published as *Where's the Water?: Water Conservation.* All new material in this edition is authored by Gail Parman.

Photo credits: Cover, p. 1 kezza/Shutterstock.com; cover, p. 1 SaltyArts Design/Shutterstock.com; cover, p. 1, 4, 6, 8, 10, 12, 14, 16, 18, 20, 21, 24 (wave) vectorstuff/Shutterstock.com; p. 4 Porstocker/Shutterstock.com; p. 5 TaylorMo/Shutterstock.com; p. 7 FOTOKITA/Shutterstock.com; p. 8 Ljupco Smokovski/Shutterstock.com; p. 9 Sudarshan Jha/Shutterstock.com; p. 11 TheRecruit/Shutterstock.com; p. 13 Alexander Knyazhinsky/Shutterstock.com; p. 15 NASA; p. 17 Rawpixel.com/Shutterstock.com; p. 19 Riccardo Mayer/Shutterstock.com; p. 20 Ahmiii24/Shutterstock.com; p. 21 Somchai Som/Shutterstock.com

Cataloging-in-Publication Data
Names: Parman, Gail.
Title: Conserving water / Gail Parman.
Description: Buffalo, New York : PowerKids Press, 2027. | Series: Water wise | Includes glossary and index.
Identifiers: ISBN 9781499458251 (pbk.) | ISBN 9781499458268 (library bound) | ISBN 9781499458275 (ebook)
Subjects: LCSH: Water conservation--Juvenile literature.
Classification: LCC TD388.P377 2027 | DDC 333.9116--dc23

Printed in China

CPSIA Compliance Information: Batch #QSPK27. For Further Information contact Rosen Publishing at 1-800-237-9932.

Contents

Wonderful Water

All living things on Earth need water. However, it's a nonrenewable **resource**, which means there's only a limited amount of it. In fact, the amount of water on Earth has been about the same for millions of years, even while the number of people on Earth continues to grow and grow.

Population growth, pollution, and **global climate change** are greatly affecting the water on Earth. That's why conserving, or caring for, Earth's water is very important. We need clean water to drink, cook, and wash. What would you do without it?

Go with the Flow

Water covers more than 70 percent of Earth's surface, but only about 1 percent of it is fresh water that can be used by people for drinking and washing.

The human population keeps growing, so the need for clean water is higher than ever.

Water Pollution

Pollution has a huge impact on Earth's water. Water can be polluted in many ways, such as litter or dirty runoff. After it rains or snows, water makes its way back into lakes and rivers. It carries dirt and trash from our streets and yards with it. It may also carry **chemicals** used on farms or in factories. This water is called runoff, and it can contaminate, or pollute, our waterways.

Runoff can carry animal and human waste into waterways too. People can get very sick if they drink water contaminated with waste.

Go with the Flow

Groundwater, or the water naturally stored underground, can also be polluted by mining waste. As mining occurs, harmful chemicals can enter the water supply.

When trash winds up in the ocean, animals may eat it and choke or become tangled in it and drown. The health of ocean **habitats** affects human life as well.

Climate Change

Climate change has a big impact on Earth's water. It is one reason why we must work to conserve water all over the world.

Climate change is causing bodies of water in some parts of the world to dry up. More than 100 countries have been losing fresh water each year. Droughts have become more and more common.

In other areas, climate change is causing glaciers to melt, which can harm the animals and plants living nearby. Some animals have too little food or have to find new homes.

Go with the Flow

The burning of **fossil fuels**, like coal, oil, and natural gas, has played a part in climate change. We use these fuels to make electricity and to power cars and other vehicles.

Global climate change is causing Earth's weather to become more **extreme**. Areas that are dry are becoming drier. Areas that are usually wet are becoming wetter.

Dangerous Droughts

Conserving water during a drought is extra important. A drought is a period of time when an area has much less **precipitation** than usual.

Local governments often make rules about how and when water is used so there isn't a shortage. But many times, conservation efforts during a drought include using groundwater. Since there's not enough precipitation to replace the groundwater, too much of this important resource may be used up in some areas. Scientists say this might cause even more problems in the future.

Go with the Flow

Droughts can cause long-term harm to an area. Dry conditions make farming harder and can lead to an increase in wildfires.

Hundreds of gallons of water a year can be wasted by leaky sinks and showers. Getting them fixed can help your family conserve water and save money too!

Reusing Water

You've probably heard the phrase "reduce, reuse, recycle," but did you know that water can be recycled too? One major water conservation effort is cleaning wastewater so that it can be used again. Wastewater is any water that's been used, such as the water that goes down the drain when you take a shower.

Wastewater treatment plants clean wastewater. However, they may not be able to remove all pollutants from the water. Scientists carefully test water to make sure it is safe for people. Keeping an eye on water **quality** is very important.

Go with the Flow

If you collect the water that you use to rinse fruits or vegetables, it can be reused to water plants or flush the toilet.

Collecting rainwater is a good way to reuse water. It can be used to water your garden during dry spells.

Space Missions

NASA (National Aeronautics and Space Administration) can monitor water changes on Earth from space. NASA's Gravity Recovery and Climate Experiment (GRACE) **mission** tracks Earth's groundwater levels using **satellites**. Scientists use this information to learn how the amount of fresh water on Earth is changing over time.

The GRACE mission, as well as its follow-on mission GRACE-FO, have been used to watch the water levels in California. It showed that since 2003, the groundwater in the Central Valley of California has gone down enough to cause concern. The amount of water in the ground there has been decreasing for more than 20 years.

Go with the Flow

The GRACE mission orbited Earth from 2002 to 2017. GRACE-FO took over in 2018.

GRACE-FO continues to monitor changes in Earth's water, including glaciers, ice sheets, and groundwater.

Laws to Help

Governments around the world are working to help conserve water by creating laws. In 1948, the U.S. government passed the Federal Water Pollution Control Act. It was the first major law to address water pollution. Since then, many other laws have been passed to keep drinking water safe.

Starting in the 1990s, the U.S. government required companies to make low-flow showerheads, sinks, and toilets. Today, these are commonly found in homes and businesses. But there's still a lot to be done in the United States to better conserve water.

Go with the Flow

Some water pipes in the country date back to the 1800s! They leak and may allow harmful matter into drinking water. However, fixing these pipes could cost trillions of dollars.

World Water Day is March 22. Each year focuses on a different topic about the importance of clean water around the world.

Growing Populations

Today, more than 8.2 billion people live on Earth, and that number keeps growing. In some parts of the world, finding clean water is a daily challenge. Some places don't have bathroom water separate from their drinking water, which can make people sick.

Groups like World Vision have been working to help all people have clean water. They've helped millions of people in Africa by digging wells there, and their work continues to grow. Building wells and teaching people about safe water and **sanitation** can save lives.

Go with the Flow
As of 2025, about 2.1 billion people do not have access to safe drinking water. That's about one out of every four people on Earth.

Clean and safe drinking water is important for staying healthy and for washing hands, cooking, and other everyday needs.

Don't Waste Water!

Conserving water is important for everyone. And there are lots of things you can do to help! Small efforts make a big difference in water conservation on Earth.

Meat and dairy products take a lot of water to produce because they come from animals that need water to live. Eating fewer meat and dairy products can help save water. So can taking a shower instead of a bath or shortening your shower by just a couple of minutes. By conserving water, you're helping your family save money too.

Go with the Flow

The average American person uses more than 80 gallons of water each day. That's enough to fill more than 1,200 glasses of water! How can you cut back on water usage?

How Much Water Does It Take . . . .

to flush a toilet? up to 3.5 gallons (13 L)

to brush your teeth? up to 5 gallons (19 L)

to take a 10-minute shower? 25 gallons (95 L)

to fill a bathtub? 70 gallons (265 L)

to fill a pool? 22,000 gallons (83,280 L)

to produce one glass of milk? 54 gallons (204 L)

Glossary

chemical: matter that can be mixed with other matter to cause changes

extreme: great or severe

fossil fuel: matter formed over millions of years from plant and animal remains that is burned for power

global climate change: long-term change in Earth's weather, caused partly by human activities such as burning oil and natural gas

habitat: the natural place where an animal or plant lives

mission: a task or job a group must perform

precipitation: rain, snow, sleet, or hail

quality: the standard or grade of something

resource: a usable supply of something

sanitation: the act or process of making something clean and free from factors that could harm health

satellite: an object that circles Earth in order to collect and send information or aid in communication

Fact Check

1. Fresh water that can be used for drinking makes up less than________ of the water on Earth.
   a. 90 percent
   b. 70 percent
   c. 1 percent

2. When did the U.S. pass the first major law to address water pollution?
   a. 1948
   b. 1990
   c. 2018

3. Which activity uses the most water?
   a. taking a bath
   b. taking a shower
   c. brushing teeth

Answers: 1. c, 2. a, 3. a

On the Internet

Water–Use It Wisely (WUIW)
https://wateruseitwisely.com/kids-teachers/
Play games and learn about the many ways you can take part in water conservation.

WaterSense for Kids
www.epa.gov/watersense/watersense-kids
Check out more ways to help save water, then take a quiz to test your knowledge.

Publisher's note to educators and parents: Our editors have carefully reviewed these websites to ensure that they are suitable for students. Many websites change frequently, however, and we cannot guarantee that a site's future contents will continue to meet our high standards of quality and educational value. Be advised that students should be closely supervised whenever they access the Internet.

Index